CW01499424

ISBN: 9798287553371
Imprint: Independently published

Table of contents: Poems and art to transform and uplift.

Table of Contents

Dedications

With special thanks to my family.

Andy, my husband.

My children

Domini, Tsarin, and George, and my grandson Demetri whose encouragement has helped me to develop myself and find my way.

The English Mystic whose encouragement helped me to grow.

The Daily Gratitude Movement.

I am truly grateful.

Note from Sarah

This collection of poems is dedicated to all who have stepped out of their power.

I hope as you read these poems they help you to step back into your power.

There is no right way or wrong way to read these poems.

Simply open the book to any page and the right poem will be waiting for you.

Visit these poems often and, as you read them, you will find you are stepping back into your power.

You will begin to feel stronger and have an inner knowing that you will be ok.

Read these poems to yourself and your loved ones.

Speak these words to yourself. These poems are for you to grow and know that you are loved.

I often say 'stepping back into your power'. It is because I believe everyone is born into this world with power and potential. For many of us, there will be a moment in our lives where we disconnect from our power - we step out of it, and that moment can really affect how our life unfolds.

Sarah Pike

Hello, I am Sarah Pike. Power Coach, Holistic Therapist, and Shamanic Practitioner.

In the early part of my life, the experiences I went through left me believing I was inadequate, I had low self-esteem, and many limiting beliefs.

All through my life, even though I do not come from a religious background, I always knew I had a deep connection to spirit.

I am grateful Spirit runs from the top of my head to the tips of my toes.

I have never craved fame or fortune, but one thing I still crave is inner peace.

This collection of poems was born from my practice of daily gratitude journaling.

I give thanks and gratitude to The Daily Gratitude Movement, a non-profit organisation on Clubhouse and FACEBOOK

I am happy to share my morning ritual with you.

Intentionally set aside the same time each morning.

Create a sacred space that is just for you. A corner of a room where you feel safe and are surrounded by your favourite things. Have a drink, safely light a candle. Choose a journal that is personal to you, and begin to write. Just write, write to yourself, write to spirit, and over time your life will change for the better by the simple act of journaling.

Each poem was written with you in mind.

IMAGINATION

Imagination is the great friend of the unknown.
Those limiting beliefs,
why, just disown

Imagination endlessly invokes and releases
power of the possibility of you.
Every version of you
is happening now.
Spirit says, 'Trust you must',
in the glory of you
each version of you is brand new.
Your potential is here,
reach out and catch hold,
everything about you is pure gold.

Your light is the presence of the divine
that keeps your life awake,
your soul awakens in the light.
Helping others to glimpse the sacred depths within you.
Your soul did not invent itself.
Your soul is a presence, a gift from the Divine.
You are a beautiful rhyme,
now is your time.

You bring all of your inner world
experience and memory
when you are here,
present in this moment.
Your life is not elsewhere,
it is totally there, reaching out before you,
so give yourself love,
give yourself care.

When you give gratitude
you bring gratitude inside of you,

the symphony of you will come into complete harmony.
When you listen to your soul, you experience rhythm and unity,
grab hold of every opportunity.

Imagination is the great friend of the unknown.
Those limiting beliefs,
well done,
because you now
disown.

Artist – Sarah Pike

SACRED ARE YOU.

Sacred are you on the day of your birth.
You are anointed King or Queen
when you decided to walk upon this earth.

You arrived here with joy,
you arrived here with
love,
you were sent here with guidance from
above.

Golden light surrounds
your beautiful head
as the
Angels
envision your
life ahead.

With achievements,
with love,
with laughter, joy
and grace,
you continue to progress
at your own special pace.

No need to worry
how life is going,
because you can choose at any moment
to experience it flowing.

When Angels draw near
Angels express their cheer
of how you turned out,
you are amazing, dear one.
Of that, there is no doubt.

You glow like a star
on its right course,
like a ray from the altar,
a spark from source.

Enjoy your special day,
the realm of the all-knowing
are applauding.
The Almighty,
the Angels are clapping and singing,
because of all the joy you are bringing.

They said to say a big thank you to you
for all that you do,
and also to say
sacred are you.

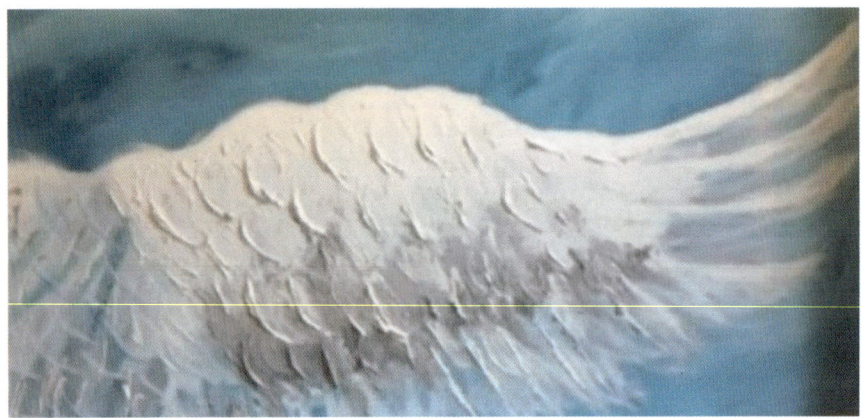

BE THE OPPORTUNITY.

Be the opportunity to ignite
your own inner sun,
in the moment,
and what is to come.

Don't you remember
we are stars wrapped up in skin,
the light you are seeking
has always been within.

The light that burns so brightly,
given to you, dear one
by the Almighty.
This light that illuminates
your soul, and
is the guiding spirit
keeping you whole,
that drives you each moment, each day.
Shining a light on your darkest days,
lighting your path, showing the way.

Be the opportunity to ignite
your own inner sun,
in the moment,
and what is to come.

Whatever you choose
you can succeed,
your success will be counted
as the sweetest seed.

Don't dally,
don't digress,
you are a beautiful work
of art in progress

Be the opportunity to ignite
your own inner sun,
in the moment,
and what is to come.

INNER AND OUTER WORLDS

As above,
so below,
as the story goes.

As within,
so without,
there can be no doubt.

However you are feeling
you have the power
to give it a new, enhanced meaning.

Life is filled
with cherished moments of love and kindness.
Remember, dear one, you are timeless.

Harmony, peace,
and abundance are in flow,
to name but a few.
These moments are here
just for you,
to help you reach out and grow.

The path you take in life
is yours to remake,
you are becoming awake.

Remember who you are,
you have come so far.

As within,
so without,
there can be no doubt

BELIEVE IN YOURSELF

Believe in yourself,
there is no one like you,
no one can hold a torch to you.

Look how far you've come.
Your journey has always been … to… become.

To become self-aware.

I know at times you have had to lay yourself bare.

To discover what serves you,
and what irks you.

Believe in yourself,
there is no one like you,
no one can hold a torch to you.

You, yes you,
have come so far,
you have battled and struggled
but……
you have raised the bar.

You are living proof
that life can change,
don't listen to others
my sisters and brothers.

The life you desire is in you,
your emotions you are feeling,
you are healing.

Believe in yourself,
keep marching towards your goal,

let me tell you,
you are already complete and whole.

Trust in
grace,
relax in the world of grace,
because you, my friend, are ace.
The time is now
to feel elation,
knock at that door,
stand tall and walk straight through it.
Be your own master
and
be your own best friend,
remember this is not the end.

Believe in yourself,
believe in you,
there is no one quite like you,
no one can hold a torch to you
or do the things that you can do,
and that is what is so special about you.

AS YOU RISE

As you rise up
may the sun bring you renewed energy by day.
As you rise may the moon magnify your light by night,
softly restore you,
and show you the way.

May the rain
gently wash away your challenges,
and pain,
as you rise again.

As you rise up
may the power of the wind and breeze
give you strength,
and bless you
with love, grace, and ease.

As you rise up
may a new way of being begin,
from living within,
seeing the world through your heart,
holding hands with others,
sisters and brothers.

No longer feeling apart,
as you walk gently through this world,
may this experience remain with you
for all the days of your life
as you rise up.

As you rise every day,
as you rise
in spite of the pain,
as you rise
don't forget your power,

getting stronger by the hour
you are living proof of gain.

You were made to live in light and glory,
this is your story.

Sarah Pike

SILENT VOICES

I hear the voices of my queen ancestors spirits calling to me,
back to the roots of my family,
reminding me to step back into the warrioress I am meant to be.

The weaving of fabric through space and time,
these warrior women of Eve let me know they are my strong bloodline.

The waters of the womb, a moment in time
when a woman is a bridge between the spiritual and physical,
birthing a spirit,
another goddess in line.

These ancestor women in the prime of their power.
The wise woman turned into a witch
by the fear of others.
The crowned one became the crone,
and subsequently lived alone.
I stand tall in their honour,
their ancient creativity I own.

With magic,
with glory,
this is now
my story.

To cut cords, release promises and contracts,
I release it all and feel enrapt.

Every story tells of a battle,
every defeat is a lesson learned,
my right to step back into
our power has been earned.

The rising of the Phoenix
has begun,
fire all around,
the ancestors watch
as the child of their line
turns out just fine.

And from them shall arise
the magnificent fiery red bird,
and at long last my queen ancestors
voices are heard.

KNOWING WHO YOU ARE

Now that I am getting to know who I am
I realise things don't always go to plan.

The path of life has many twists,
stops, and starts,
and more than the odd turn.
I take many different paths.
I now tell myself it's ok,
that's how I learn.
I have so much time,
life is the soul's
beautiful rhyme.

Time is a construct
of the human mind,
keeping us all in a bind.
Life is seen to flow as a
straight line,
from past to future.
This is an illusion,
time is vast,
full of infinite potential,
nothing is ever inconsequential.

I learn from past mistakes,
I clear off that shelf,
and stop being so hard on myself.

Perceptions over perceptions
ended with misunderstanding.
Communications
living in spirits light,
and finding my way
gives me a rich life.

Every single day
bringing me back to adoration
of life,
of love
for all things,
and all others,
my sisters and brothers.

I choose to make the best of my mistakes.
It's all an experience.
I take responsibility,
no hostility.
I still have availability
to live in stability.

Judging too quickly,
giving up so easily,
is not for me.
That's not how Great Spirit
intended my life to be.

I believe in the power of love,
after all, we're sent from above
with love.

With love, I am given second chances
with each day,
if I choose to look the right way
my life enhances.

Now that I am getting to know myself,
I am the power,
it is my story.
In love and light
I am living proof
of Great Spirits delight,
love, abundance, and glory.

THE PRESENT MOMENT

The present moment is the product of events
that have their origin in the past.
Just like the fruit is the product of the seed
that grew into a tree,
addressing our need.

There is a natural movement of events in the world.
We can see it in the phenomena
as the tide,
the ebb and flow
of the oceans and the rivers that rise up from the earth
then flows into the sea,
a natural movement towards a certain
destination, effortlessly.

The cycle of life's
Unification,
Interconnectedness,
a sense of continuum,
look how far you've come.

We are the cycle of life,
evolving self,
ever changing,
being in good health.

The present moment is the product of events
that have their origins in the past.
Just like the fruit is the product of the seed
that grew into a tree,
addressing our need.

All paths lead to spirit,
getting to choose,
is it a path of suffering, wisdom, bliss, or loss?
Be sure you pick the path to your heart.
It's always your choice,
you are the boss.

The present moment is the product of events
that have their origins in the past.
Just like the fruit is the product of the seed
that grew into a tree,
addressing our need.

WISHES HOLD

Wishes hold
a special magic
for those who dream,
life is a gift as it starts
to unfold

Wishes are a mix
of magic and love,
all given freely to us from up above.
Sometimes we must look beyond the dream,
life isn't as first it may seem.

Life makes a surprise,
radiating with vision of light,
to dream to delight,
to ensure many fun-filled hours,
through day and night.

Evoking the divine,
those dreams and wishes
are waiting to be caught,
to be present to where life is.
Remember life is short.

Wishes hold a special magic
for those who dream
THE MAGICK.

Be optimistic,
you are the magic,
the mystic,
life is a gift
as it starts to unfold,
the power has always been there,
stand strong, be bold.

A host of angels do surround,
you think at first they can't be heard or seen,
but if you listen carefully you will hear a sound,
they are all around.

This isn't your final chance,
grab those wishes and dreams,
begin to dance.
You are a shooting star,
believe how wonderful you are.

A life significant
in this instance,

a wink,

then it is gone,
so cherish.

Your spirit is replenished, your dreams are wishes.
You will come through without a blemish.

HOME

Where is your home?
Your home is inside of you.
The false belief of needing four walls
is keeping you stuck,
having you believe
you have no luck.

You are the centre of your own world and universe,
let life dance with you,
let life swirl you up
in kindness and love.
Release your flair
with confidence and dare,
to show how much you care.

Let me tell you,
yourself is not lost or left on the shelf,
become grounded, take a breath.

You have purpose
and a mission,
no permission
is required,
only self-love
is to be given.

Where is your home?
Your home is inside of you.
In your thoughts actions and deeds.
You are so powerful,
see yourself through the darkness,
see yourself in the light,
conscious voices
make better choices.

Where is your home?
Your home is inside of you.
You are always the rising balance,
the yin and the yang,
serenity and peace,
watch your power return and increase.

At times, peace and rest
is the only way to feather your mental nest.

Where is your real home?
Your real home is inside of you.
Your heart,
your being,
your home is inside of you,
the very essence of you.

Your intuition has no fears,
listening to your intuition
is the best,
it's how you feather your heart's nest.

Where is your home?
Your home is inside of you.
It's up to you
if you see rainbows,
or if you feel blue.

EYES WIDE OPEN

Eyes wide open,
no longer shrinking,
no longer feeling small.
It's time for life,
to give it your all,
whatever you say or do
remember it's your call.

Whatever you are experiencing
this is just a point of tribulation,
and nothing more.
Believe in yourself
without stipulation.

Stand up straight,
adjust your gait,
don't drag your feet.
Eye to eye
everyone you meet.
Your beautiful smile
naturally appears
to everyone you greet.

This is a point of freedom
where you walk freely
into your mission.
You don't need permission to grow,
to shine,
to rise up,
you are the light,
you are the glory,
this is your story.

Sarah Pike

A golden cord
has always been attached to you,
it's always been pulled tight.
This golden cord has never wavered,
this connection to you
proves you are favoured,
life is here to be savoured.

You are motivational
and inspirational,
independent of glitches,
don't you know your soul
is full of wonder and riches.

Eyes wide open,
no longer shrinking,
no longer feeling small,
life is short.

Life is waiting,
give it your all,
it's yours
and only your call.

IMPORTANT MUSCLES

The muscle of the heart,
it is the seat of the soul from where love and wisdom flows,
and intuition grows.

I sense and feel my world around me,
it is a world where I want to be.

The muscle of my mind
that allows me to imagine,
to dream, to create, to comfort, to encourage, and soothe.

The muscle of my body,
my arms to hug tighter,
my hands to hold hands longer,
my legs to walk many miles next to others,
my sisters and brothers.

My ears to listen,
my eyes to see,
I now gratefully receive love and comfort.
My new learning of acceptance
is a magical thing,
I now feel and believe
I am connected to everything.

My muscle of journaling,
my muscle of writing, a quiet time
with lit candle helps me feel fine.
Wisdom is in all of us.
Wisdom, it is sublime.

My muscle of meditation,
consideration, and contemplation.

My muscle of the rhyming word,
spoken into the universe.
I write what I seek,
I am no longer meek.

Morning glory,
this is my story.

PRECIOUS LIFE

So precious is our life on this earth,
from the very start,
the moment of our birth.

Life is filled with ups and downs,
days of laughter,
days of frowns.

The best of life
is yet to come,
living a life,
maybe
inner peace
has just begun.

Travelling so far
to learn who we are.

Through life's ups and downs
ourselves we can defend,
being firmly on the mend,
realising we are a beautiful mixture,
a splendid blend.

Life is filled with ups and downs,
days of laughter,
days of frowns.

Through these days of ups and downs,
stormy or fine,
these precious days
are still yours and mine.

Life at times is like a rollercoaster ride,
there are times to let go,
to ride the storm,
to go with the flow.
It will pass,
it's a ride,
if this rule
we abide.

After every dip
there follows an ascent,
our spirit does revive,
as we continue this eventful ride.

The best of life
is yet to come,
living a life,
maybe
inner peace
has just begun.

Life is filled with ups and downs,
days of laughter,
days of frowns.

But just like on that rollercoaster
we must hold tight,
because life is life,
and we're here
to take flight after flight.

NEW BEGINNING

Each day is a new beginning, you will die many times in one life,
and you will create yourself anew.
This is natural,
this is a gift,
remember you have the power and choice to uplift.

Don't abandon yourself,
not when you're sick,
not when you're tired,
not when you've lost the thread.
The thought or thing
that keeps you awake at night,
when you toss and turn in your bed,
don't be misled.

The person you were has gone.
Let's celebrate,
you've been reborn.
Great spirit says
stop feeling forlorn.

Throw that old skin
into the water or up to the sky,
as you step into what wants to emerge
gather yourself up
and fly high.
You have nothing to lose,
so give it a try.

Each day is a new beginning, you will die many times in one life,
and you will create yourself anew.
This is natural,
this is a gift,
remember you have the power and choice to uplift.

Nothing can hold you back when you are willing to be yourself
every day.
You're given the message,
this is your story,
so sparkle and shimmer as you
step into your glory.
Leave behind what doesn't serve you,
it's time to stop,
pause within,
then take that first step
for your new life to begin.

It's time to release
what no longer serves you,
you were meant for bigger things,
now is the time to begin.

Close that chapter,
shake off your past, don't waste your life,
it doesn't last.
Thrust yourself into living,
hold on to great spirit
who has whispered
in your ear,
and blown away the dust.
Look up,
smile,
and say I trust.

THE CYCLE OF THE EARTH

The cycle of the Earth,
the natural world.
Those beautiful four Seasons,
to be aligned
to grow.
Nature teaches us how to be in flow.

Father Sky,
Mother Earth.

Since the day of my birth,
not knowingly,
I have danced to the sound of another's drum.

Sometimes it's loud,
sometimes it's a quiet hum.

With the sun rises creation,
Earth's mesmerising visual,
the gentle breeze scatters limiting thoughts,
freshwater cleansing eyes,
seeing from within a new powerful life is about to begin.

Strong foundations that go deep into Mother Earth,
thick green roots are big and strong,
an inner knowing is sensed right here,
right now, is where I belong.

In harmony with the natural world.
Earth's keeper
of each and every soul.
I am and always will be complete and whole.

Sarah Pike

Abundant power
getting stronger by the hour.
The inner eye can see again,
it's not just a reflection through a window pane.

When I look back at my own life,
I realise I have always had my power,
I am the decider
every single moment, every hour.

I now powerfully dance to the sound
of my own beautiful drum.
The beat is getting stronger and stronger,
louder and louder, no longer a distant hum.

The life I wish to live
has finally begun.

THE SPIRIT REBORN

The spirit reborn
as a sacred work of art,
the stars chart a new start,
as love is all around,
bursting from our hearts.
A powerful knowing is to be believed
with this new life conceived.

Across the vales expanse where spirits roam,
a journey is taken,
all is not lost,
to bring the wandering essence of love back home,
where on this path, beautiful, powerful seeds are sown.

The heart charts love
that is embedded deep.
A constellation of angels,
a host of light,
gives us strength
to feel our might.

Beneath the moon's soft glow,
the whispering leaves
make a mellow bed
to lay a weary head.
While the river gently flows
glistening silver,
love is felt with a quiver.

Through the winds that bring tales
of ancient stories to be told,
love seeks and weaves the threads of light, winning over dark
such stories to behold.

A gentle call to mend within
each piece restored,
the soul once more,
with healing chants,
the journey to heal
within can begin.

The spirit reborn
as a sacred work of art,
the stars chart a new start,
as love is all around
bursting from our hearts.
A powerful knowing is to be believed
with this new life conceived.

BEING GRATEFUL

Being grateful for everything I've got
shows me how rich I am, I have a lot.

I am grateful for all family
that comes my way,
teaching me how to be
day by day.

Family doesn't have to be blood,
the blood of the covenant
is stronger than the waters of the womb.
With the right circle
the rhythm of life keeps me in fine tune.

I'm grateful for the rain,
it waters my soul.
I feel no pain
it's all for my gain.

Being grateful for everything I've got
shows me how rich I am, I have a lot.

I'm grateful for the stars
that fill the upper skies,
illuminating with the moon
the beauty and riches of Mother Earth, I experience
no doom.

Instead,
a constellation of angels
comes my way,
they rearrange my heart,
feeling stronger,
no longer
falling apart.

These angels
sing and dance,
right here by my side.
These angels are you,
Earth angels, everyone,
with your listening ears,
hearts full of love,
whenever I am with you
I say goodbye to my fears.

Being grateful for everything I've got
shows me how rich I am.
I do indeed have a lot.

SUNSHINE

Be in the sunshine of your life.
'Roar'
as you explore,
you are not poor,
don't limit your being
it's richness you're seeing.

Be the sunshine of your life,
your heart
is a powerful gift,
a blessing,
use it to heal any rift and uplift.
Being deeper in your heart,
all the challenges,
all sadness,
will depart.
Your soul is
Great Spirits' abode,
release any heavy load.

Great Spirit, your presence we seek,
with you life is not bleak,
we are powerful, not meek.

Be the sunshine of your life.
'Roar'
as you explore,
you are not poor,
don't limit your being,
it's richness you're seeing.

Love and blessings
light your day,
angels are with you
every twist and turn,
every step of the way.

When you smile
it's like a morning in spring,
you can hear the ancestors sing.

The light that you are,
your beauty imprints,
your presence is felt,
a life well lived is part of your blueprints.
Remember to ground yourself,
it's good for your health,
doing this
you'll find your internal wealth.

You are the light,
it was given to you
as your birthright.

Using your light well,
in harmony
you shall dwell,
and in stature you swell.

Be the sunshine of your life.
'Roar'
as you explore,
you are not poor,
don't limit your being,
it's richness you're seeing.

THIS SOUL CALLED YOU

This soul called you,
you can't be replaced.
With love you are graced.
You have come with a mission,
you have travelled so far,
now is the time to remember who you are,
looking forward with a vision.

You are a wish fulfilment
in a life full of chaos,
you are the blessing of stillment.

You are an answered prayer,
life happening all at once,
an abundance of love
I do declare.

You are a gift from the divine, your divinity and sovereignty
is not a novelty.
You are the magic that people dream about,
you are the love that souls search for.
You are abundance personified,
you are to be glorified.

A golden light in the darkest night,
leaving the dark and entering the light,
angels celebrated on the day of your birth,
you are the one who brings out the beauty on Earth.

You are the reminder of the goodness in this world,
don't let other people's wounds
and distortions sway you from this truth.
You are divine love,
of this you need no proof.

This soul called you,
you can't be replaced.
With love you are graced.
You have come with a mission,
you have travelled so far,
now is the time to remember who you are,
looking forward with a vision.

Sarah Pike

GARDENERS OF THE SOIL

I am a gardener of the soil,
it's where I love to tend and toil.
But there are many other gardeners
who come in different guises,
whose hearts are huge in sizes

The gardener who holds the hands of our children,
who makes sure they are loved
that they have a mission and a vision.

Gardeners who look after our elders,
who make sure their dignity is intact,
a work of love and that is a fact

Gardeners come in all shapes and sizes.
They are angels as humans
sent from above
to bring joy, peace, harmony,
and, above all else, love.

These gardeners are the flowers,
their smiles are the petals.
Each petal is a kind word
to encourage, to motivate.
These kinds of gardeners
are not rare
but they're special,
because of their love and care.

I celebrate these gardeners,
as their love influences
the world,
this Earth,
and I thank SPIRIT
for giving them life and birth,
to walk and love on our beautiful mother Earth

YOU RECEIVE WHAT YOU SEED

Something only lives as long as we remember it,
it only has power if we feed it.

No longer feed doubt,
no longer feed fear.
Doing this keeps you grounded
in a moment,
always present,
always here,
thinking clear.
Set an intention to feed the daily practice of gratitude,
life changes in an instant
by huge magnitude.

I am a storyteller and a poet of a different kind,
my stories are here to help calm the mind.

I tell stories of ancestors.
Earth, wind, air, and fire.
I am the tiger
who roams freely
ascending higher and higher.

But my sisters and brothers,
so are you.
Your experiences,
your wisdom,
your stories of life,
you must share.
It's OK for your soul to bear
and tell that story
of achievement and power
over despair.

You are a winner.
Your new way of being
is not just a glimmer,
you have returned to stand in your power
every single moment, every hour.

Become the curator
of your own future.
Be the person Spirit knew and moulded,
before he placed you in your mother's womb.
Remember the seeds and dreams
SPIRIT gifted your soul,
you are already complete and whole.

We receive in life what we seed,
something only lives as long as we remember it.

Feed your strength,
your kindness, wisdom, and love.
Rise like the phoenix you are,
that has been sent with love
from the highest
great Spirit
from above.

Something only lives as long as we remember it,
it only has power if we feed it.

Sarah Pike

MAKE THE CHANGE

Make the change,
move to a new height.
Make the change,
use all of your SPIRIT given might.

Life as we know it
can sometimes get rough,
make the change
through SPIRIT.
SPIRIT will never leave you
when things get tough.

Change is upon us,
change upon change.
With spring soaring
in abundance
life's stream
is flowing,
a gentle breeze of change
is blowing.
Can you feel
possibilities showing up and glowing.

Nothing is permanent,
change happens all the time.
New beginnings,
a new start.
This is the season
of reaffirmation,
the change can be
bountiful, beautiful,
and plentiful.

Make the change,
move to a new height.
Make the change,
use all of your SPIRIT given might.

At times there can be confusion
in life's cycle.
When change occurs
don't be afraid,
change can herald
a happy conclusion.

REDIRECTION IS CREATION

Imagination is the beginning of redirection
and creation.
Imagination is intuition
without hesitation,
a knowing
life is glowing,
beautifully flowing.

Let your flame roar
and shine bright.
Creation and redirection
are now in force,
you can feel it
with all of your might.
Let your intuition wrap around you
like a warm cloak at night.

Imagination comes from the creator
those remembered,
trailing wisps of majesty
and sovereignty
of who you really are.
You are inspiring
as you honour yourself,
this is your story
as you redirect yourself,
and step back into your glory.

Ancient wisdom
courses through your veins.
Insight and intuition
alleviating any pains,
cosmic connections
abound for your reflections.

A twist of fate,
a happy miracle,
balanced karma,
life is at the pinnacle.

Like the seed
that comes forth in spring,
Mother Earth
has allowed new life to begin.
Take hold of a self-realisation
of circumstance,
as transformation comes
from within.

Imagination is the beginning of redirection
and creation.
Imagination is intuition
without hesitation,
a knowing
life is glowing,
beautifully flowing.

AWAY FROM THE DIN

There is a place deep within,
away from all the din.
This place is way deeper
beneath the skin,
a stillness is known,
life is good
without the spin.

Peace within,
is it time to begin?
To let go,
to speak of peace,
no anger,
no doubt,
allowing to release.
A soul finds peace
and doesn't care,
when this place is reached
harmony is there.

Peace is part of
great spirits gift,
any time, any place.
That inner love
a sanctuary is found,
a calm space
to uplift
in this place.
Spirit gifted us grace.

The wind is blowing gently
as a page of life's chapter
flutters in the breeze.
Recognition is found,
along with laughter,
life cheers on the adapter.

Another page,
a new story begins.
Busy making plans and amends,
feeling whispers of good intent.
Letting go of it all,
it never made sense,
inner peace comes forth,
no recompense.

The sun shines,
calming the breeze.
Caressing faces,
those burdens have gone.
Joy and contentment,
are challenges replacements.

There is a place deep within.
This place is way deeper beneath the skin,
a stillness is known,
life is good without the spin,
away from all the din.

PARTS OF ME

Parts of me had to be the death of me,
so as I could be reborn
the me I am meant to be.

I have no need or time
for those thoughts that keep swirling in my head,
stopping me from getting up from my bed.

I have no need or time
for those rubbish emotions,
that keep me bound and stuck.
I have no need or time,
I am and have always been just fine.

I put down my shield and sword,
I know I'm not really of this world.

At the end of the day
when I rest my head,
the challenges I've won,
in my heart I know
I've done my best.

Parts of me had to be the death of me,
so as I could be reborn
the me I am meant to be.

Spirit gave me life,
to love and care,
to honour myself,
honour my sisters and brothers.
I am not here to be small,
because if that were true,
what would be the point of it all.

Like the rose bush in flower
I cut back all dead wood.
I stepped back into my power,
releasing the blighted leaves and wood
I get stronger by the hour.

I am in alignment
with the Ying and the Yang,
the feminine and the masculine.
This lifetime isn't long,
it goes just like that
with a bang.

I am gifted every day,
spirit always shows me the way.
To climb that imagined high mountain,
that is nothing more than a small fountain.

Part of me had to be the death of me,
so as I could be reborn
the me I am meant to be.

I am reborn,
I stand in my power.
Being the best of me,
I can always be
living in the Kingdom and the realm
of anything and everything is possible.
It's all up to me
if I want it to be.
I am living my life,
I'm taking the helm.
The environment I live in
is healthy and good.
I am all in,
my new life can begin.

I come back stronger,
I was no longer
who I used to be.
From the darkness I learned who I wasn't meant to be,
I learned who I am,
I am stronger.

Part of me had to be the death of me,
so as I could be reborn
the me I am meant to be.

In being reborn
magic gives a light to miracles,
seeing life through wonder and awe.
We are the emissary of light,
focusing on the light,
radiant and transformational.
We are vibrant
and sensational.

FORGIVENESS

Today I choose forgiveness,
to forgive myself.
I forgive the misdeeds of yesterday.
I do not let it mar my today,
for it will stop me
from building or finding my way.

I am a being of love,
I must learn to let go,
I forgive, no longer misgive.

Not allowing the pain
to return again,
so much learning to gain.

Forgiveness puts an end to the past,
the dark wings of night,
those moments tell us
this too shall pass,
they will take flight.
Remember we are the light,
everything is temporary,
nothing will last,
as powerful positive emotions are cast.

In forgiveness
new hope arises.
A brightness in the heart,
a new birth,
a surprise,
a life moving forward, new dreams being fulfilled.
Life bursting with goodness at the seams

Not to forgive
is an emptiness,
a lonely lost essence.
Forgiveness is a place to visit,
to reclaim your soul,
and bring back a strong presence.

Forgiveness is cathartic and noble,
shedding the light on all that's good.
Practising forgiveness
in your power you are stood.

When forgiveness is shown,
the journey is seen.
How life is so rich,
as a stroll under the stars,
or driving fast cars,
a magnificent healing, oh what a feeling.

Today I choose forgiveness,
to forgive myself.
I forgive the misdeeds of yesterday.
I do not let it mar my today,
for it will stop me
from building or finding my way.

Sarah Pike

SACRED LEARNINGS

Things I have learned.
I have learned that if you let your light shine,
to be your true self,
your love and ideas
will never be left on the shelf.

I have learned
that challenges appear,
that this too shall pass,
I am never alone
as angels draw near.

I have learned
no matter how deep the sorrow,
there is always hope
the sun will shine tomorrow.

I have learned
I am free,
if I just allow myself to be.

I have learned
that hearts break,
and hearts might ache,
but spirit can heal them all,
when tears fall.

I have learned
there is a right ending for everything,
and a beautiful new beginning.
Days bring sunlight
leading to dark,
light a candle as an offering.
Give thanks to spirit,
dreams really do come true.
Life at any moment
can start anew.

I know for a fact
a golden cord
has always been attached to you and me.
Great spirit pulls tight
as together we walk in great spirit's light.
This golden cord has never wavered.
This connection to you and me proves we are favoured,
life is here to be savoured.

I have learned it's such a pleasure
to do life with others,
especially you,
my sisters and brothers.

EVERY HURDLE OVERCOME

Every hurdle overcome,
every tear dried,
shapes us into something stronger,
wiser, beautiful inside.

Embrace the storms,
don't set a limit.
They reveal the resilience
of your spirit.

No longer forlorn,
looking for reasons
why you were born.
No affliction,
only affection,
drying tears,
releasing fears.

Every hurdle overcome,
every tear dried,
shapes us into something stronger,
wiser, beautiful inside.

Everything and everyone
has their own season,
life is sometimes quirky,
without rhyme or reason.

Step into your new story,
own your glory.
Let the past go,
as contentment arrives,
tell yourself you know
your heart will lift.
As you remember
you are the gift,
you have flown,
the time is now.
Witness that which you have sown,
see how much you have grown.

NONE OF US KNOW HOW MUCH TIME WE HAVE LEFT

None of us know how much time we have left.
Time is elapsing,
those rules and boundaries that were created
are now collapsing.

Life is an adventure to be lived.
We can change our direction in an instant,
life is no longer far off in the distant.

Like the frog on the lily pad,
jumping from one lily pad to the other.
Maybe a particular lily pad is not meant for you
but you still have to jump.
Otherwise, how would you know,
don't limit experiences,
that's how to grow.

Life is an adventure,
the good and the bad,
the dark and the light,
remember you are a delight.

Your words and actions
have the power to uplift and ignite.

The bad times help show us we are not
paying attention to the riches we already possess.
Pay attention to your own special finesse,
spirit gave you life for you to bless.

You have and will continue to grow,
you still have bagfuls of seeds left to sew.
Scatter them well in different directions,
for that is how you will find the right connections.

You have Divine heritage and a sacred destiny,
you were created to live life in ecstasy.

The area around your heart is Holy Land,
where the soul dwells
and expands.

By being kind,
by being true,
life's bountiful moments
will flow in abundance,
especially for you.

Printed in Dunstable, United Kingdom

Rhythms of Life

A book of empowering
poetry
By Sarah Pike

Rhythms of Life

A small but mighty book of empowering poetry.

Poetry is the essence of life that washes away from the soul the dust of everyday challenges.

When the heart hurts, it is asking for the breath to be back in the present moment.

This collection of poems strengthens the reader and brings him or her back to the present moment.

Written and illustrated by Sarah Pike